YOUNG DISCOVERER

# RIVERS AND OCEANS

## BARBARA TAYLOR

## KINGFISHER
NEW YORK

KINGFISHER
Larousse Kingfisher Chambers Inc.
80 Maiden Lane
New York, New York 10038
www.kingfisherpub.com

First American edition published in 1993
10 9 8 7 6 5 4 3 2 1

1TR/1201/WKT/- (RNB)/128MA

LIBRARY OF CONGRESS CATALOGING-IN-
PUBICATION DATA
Taylor, Barbara.
  Rivers and oceans / Barbara Taylor.—
1st ed.
    p.   cm.—(Young discoverers)
  Includes index.
  Summary: Introduces the different forms
of water in our world; the water cycle;
stages in the life of a river; ocean currents;
waves and tides; lakes; water pollution.
  1. Rivers—Juvenile literature.  2. Ocean
—Juvenile literature [1. Rivers.  2. Ocean]
I. Title.  II. Series: Taylor, Barbara.
Young discoverers.
GB1203.8.T39   1993
551.48'3—dc20  92-28421  CIP AC

ISBN 0-7534-5508-0

Series editor: Sue Nicholson
Series and cover design: Terry Woodley
Design: Ben White
Picture research: Elaine Willis
Cover illustration: Chris Forsey
Illustrations: Hayward Art Group pp.4 (top),
  5 (top), 6 (bottom), 8 (left), 9 (top), 12 (top right
  and bottom left), 14 (left), 22-23, 24 (bottom
  right), 25 (top); Kevin Maddison pp.4-5 (bottom),
  6 (top), 8 (bottom), 10-11, 12 (bottom), 14-21,
  23 (bottom right), 24 (top), 25 (bottom), 26
  (bottom), 28, 29 (left), 30 (bottom left), 31 (right);
  Janos Marffy, Kathy Jakeman Illustration pp.7, 8
  (top right), 9 (bottom), 11 (top), 13, 15 (top
  right), 18 (right), 23 (top), 24 (bottom left), 27,
  30, 31; Simon Tegg, Simon Girling & Associates
  pp.26 (top), 29 (right)
Photographs: Harold Berger p.10, Alan Cork p.19,
  Dennis Gilbert p.29, Hutchinson Library pp.15,
  16, 20; ZEFA p.13

Printed in Hong Kong

# About This Book

This book tells you about rivers, lakes, and oceans and how they shape the land. It also gives you lots of ideas for projects and things to look out for. You should be able to find nearly everything you need to do the projects around your home. You may need to buy some items, but they are all cheap and easy to find. Be careful when you are studying a river out of doors. Do not go near rivers, lakes, or any open water on your own — always go with an adult.

## Activity Hints

- Before you begin, read the instructions carefully and collect all the things you need.
- When you have finished, clear everything away, especially sharp things like knives and scissors, and wash your hands.

- Start a special notebook. Keep a record of what you do in each project and the things that you find out.

# Contents

 **Water in Our World**  4

 **The Water Cycle**  6

 **Water Under the Ground**  8

 **Rivers of Ice**  10

 **River Sources**  12

 **Rivers at Work**  13

 **Rushing Rivers**  14

 **Winding Rivers**  16

 **The Nile**  19

 **Lakes**  20

 **Oceans and Seas**  22

 **Waves, Currents, and Tides**  24

 **Waves at Work**  26

 **Water Pollution**  29

 **Amazing Rivers and Oceans**  31

**Index**  32

# Water in our World

Almost three-fourths of the Earth's surface is covered with water, making the planet look blue from space. Water is essential to life on Earth. Without it, all animals and plants would die. Oceans and seas make up most of the world's water. They contain salty water. Water that is not salty — fresh water — comes from rain which fills our ponds, streams, lakes, and rivers. Water is also trapped in glaciers, or rivers of ice, and in huge blocks of ice, called icebergs.

How much water do you use every day? In North America and Europe, each person uses over two bathtubs full. In Asia, people use much less.

stream

### 👁 Eye-Spy

Do you live near a stream or a river, or even by the ocean? Why not start a scrapbook about it. Paste in photographs or drawings to show its wildlife and how people use the water.

Many rivers start in hills and mountains as small, fast-flowing streams. As the water rushes downhill, it cuts deep valleys through the land.

In the middle part of a river, the water flows more slowly in a wide, flat valley. The river curves from side to side in loops called meanders.

Arctic
Ocean

Yenisei    Lena

Mackenzie — Great
                        Lakes

Ganges                    Lake
                                Baikal

Mississippi               Atlantic
                                Ocean
                                                Nile

Pacific                    Amazon          Indian
Ocean                                        Ocean

                                                        Darling

                    Southern
                    (Antarctic)
                    Ocean

## Where is Our Water?

About 97 percent of the world's water is salty and is found in our oceans and seas. The other 3 percent is fresh water, from ice (in glaciers and ice sheets), rivers and lakes, or clouds (see page 6).

clouds

rivers and lakes

ice

oceans and seas

The map above shows the Earth's oceans and its major rivers and lakes. The biggest and deepest ocean is the Pacific. The longest river is the Nile (see page 19).

lake

meanders          delta

sea

Where it meets the sea, a river drops, or deposits, the mud and soil it carries and may build up a flat tongue of land called a delta.

5

# The Water Cycle

Did you know that the total amount of water on Earth is the same as it was over 4 billion years ago? This is because water rains down from the sky then rises up again in a never-ending journey called the water cycle. The Sun heats the liquid water in rivers, lakes, and oceans, turning some of it into an invisible gas called water vapor. The water vapor evaporates, or disappears, into the air. If the air rises and cools down, the water vapor condenses, or turns back, into droplets of liquid water.

Try marking the edge of a puddle with chalk, string, or a row of pebbles to see how long it takes for the water to evaporate. Do puddles dry up faster in the sunshine or in the shade?

## Water All Around

Water falls from clouds as rain or snow (1) and collects in rivers, lakes, seas, and oceans (2). The Sun's heat turns some water into water vapor in the air (3). The air rises and cools and some water vapor turns back into liquid water, forming clouds (4).

# Do it yourself

**Plants take up water through their roots and give off water through their leaves. If you grow plants in a sealed jar, they will be able to use the same water over and over again, just like the Earth's real water cycle.**

**3.** Put the top on the bottle and leave it in a shady place.

**4.** See how water given off by the plants condenses on the cool sides of the bottle and runs down into the soil. The plants can use the water again and again.

## More Things to Try

Ask an adult to hold a spoon in the jet of steam from a boiling kettle. Watch how water condenses on the cold spoon to form droplets — just like the raindrops falling from clouds.

oven glove

spoon tied to the end of a stick

drops of water

**1.** Place a large plastic bottle on its side and spoon in a layer of gravel with a layer of good soil on top.

**2.** Use thin sticks to push small plants, such as ivy, ferns, and mosses, into the soil. Press down the soil around the plants with a thread spool tied to a stick.

# Water Under the Ground

Some of the water that falls as rain soaks into the ground, slowly trickling down through tiny air spaces in soil or through cracks in rocks. Eventually, the water reaches a layer of rock — called impermeable rock — that will not allow water to pass through it. The rocks just above this impermeable rock layer become soaked with water, forming pockets or reservoirs of water called aquifers. The highest level of water in an aquifer is called the water table.

 **Eye-Spy**

A sponge soaks up water easily because it is full of holes. In a similar way, soils and some rocks contain air spaces which easily fill up with water.

Water easily wears away soft rocks like limestone, forming tunnels and caves. As water drips through cave roofs, it evaporates, leaving behind rocky pillars called stalactites and stalagmites.

stalactite

stalagmite

## Desert Oases

In a desert, it hardly ever rains. However, moist areas called oases are found in places where water-filled rocks are near the Earth's surface. The water may have soaked into mountains hundreds of miles away, draining down through the rocks under the desert.

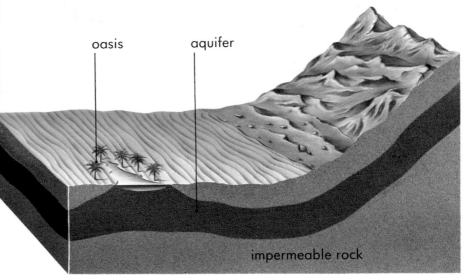

oasis

aquifer

impermeable rock

# Do it yourself

**Try making your own stalactites and stalagmites. You need two jars, a saucer, yarn, washing soda, and water.**

**1.** Fill the jars with warm water and stir in plenty of washing soda, making sure that all the soda dissolves, or disappears, in the water.

**2.** Stand the jars in a warm, safe place with the saucer between them.

**3.** Loop a piece of yarn from one jar to the other so that each end can soak up the water.

washing soda

yarn

warm water

**4.** As the water slowly evaporates, bits of soda will be left behind, dripping down to form a narrow pillar.

# Rivers of Ice

In areas where there is snow all year round, water may be frozen into huge ice sheets or "rivers of ice," called glaciers. Glaciers can be up to 250 miles (400 km) long and are often 1,000 feet (300 m) thick. They form when piles of snow are squashed together to make ice — in the same way that a snowball goes hard when you press it tightly. The ice in a glacier becomes thick and heavy and slides slowly downhill.

The bottom end of a glacier is called its snout. Here it is warmer, so the ice melts to form streams of icy water called meltwater.

Glaciers start high up in mountains or near the North and South Poles where it is very cold. Snow piles up in layers and is squashed and frozen into ice.

As the glacier moves slowly downhill, it grinds and scrapes the land beneath, carrying away rocks and boulders and gouging out a deep, wide valley.

The ice on the surface of a glacier is brittle, like taffy. As the glacier moves, the ice can snap, forming jagged pinnacles and deep cracks called crevasses.

# Do it yourself

**See how the pieces of rock carried by a glacier scrape against the land beneath, creating a force called friction which slows the glacier down.**

Make two blocks of ice as shown on the right. Which "glacier" moves more slowly when you slide it down the slope?

water

gravel and water

## Eye-Spy

The pieces of rock carried by a glacier make its sides and bottom rough. Glaciers smooth and polish the rocks they move over in the same way that a rough nail file smooths a broken fingernail.

## After the Ice

After glaciers have melted, we can find clues that tell us where they used to be. These include hollows with steep walls (called cirques) and deep U-shaped valleys.

cirque

U-shaped valley

snout

11

# River Sources

The source or beginning of most rivers is rainwater that collects in small hollows or gullies and trickles over the surface of the land. This water does not soak into the soil or the rocks below because the rocks are either already full of water or will not let water pass through them. The trickles of water join up into a stream and several streams flow together to make a river. Other rivers start as mountain springs (see the box on the right) or flow from lakes, marshes, or glaciers.

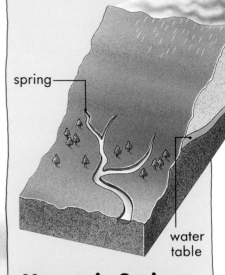

## Mountain Springs

Rainwater may collect under the ground, above impermeable rock layers through which it cannot pass. Where these rock layers reach the surface, the water above gushes out as a mountain spring.

Many rivers begin in natural hollows, which fill up with water to form ponds or lakes.

## Source of the Nile

The world's longest river is the Nile. Its main source is Lake Victoria in Uganda, Africa. The river flows north through Sudan and Egypt to the Mediterranean Sea. See page 19 for more about the Nile River.

# Rivers at Work

Streams and rivers have the power to change the shape of the land. But water on its own is not strong enough to wear land away. It is all the boulders, pebbles, and grains of sand carried along by the water that give a river its cutting force. Sometimes, however, swirling water may split rocks apart by forcing air into cracks in the rock. Some rocks may also be eaten away by chemicals carried in water.

Over millions of years, the Colorado River in Arizona has carved out a huge channel called the Grand Canyon.

## Do it yourself

**Make your own river and see how it carves out a path downhill.**

**1.** Outside, build a sloping mountain out of damp sand, pebbles, and mud.

**2.** Slowly pour a steady stream of water over the top of the mountain. Watch carefully to see how the water finds the quickest way down the slope and how much sand and gravel it carries.

damp sand and gravel

13

# Rushing Rivers

At the start of its course, a river flows quickly, ripping up loose stones and pebbles and hurling them at the sides and bed of the river. After a storm, a river often contains more water, so it is able to pick up and carry huge boulders. With this material, called its load, the river pounds away at the land, cutting downward to form a steep-sided valley shaped like the letter V. This part of a river's course often has waterfalls and rapids — stretches of very fast-flowing water.

## A Waterfall is Born

Different kinds of rock wear away at different speeds. So where water flows over bands of soft rock and hard rock (1), the soft rock is worn away first, leaving a step of hard rock (2). Over thousands of years, more soft rock is worn away and the step becomes steeper (3). The water tumbles over the step as a waterfall.

The photograph on the opposite page shows the spectacular waterfalls on the Iguacu River, on the borders of Brazil and Argentina in South America.

① 

hard rock

② 

③

The drawing below shows the round dips or holes that you can often see in a dry river bed. These potholes are formed when water swirls pebbles round and round, wearing out hollows. The water swirls faster as the hollows get deeper.

pothole

### 👁 Eye-Spy

Put some gravel in a clear plastic container then hold it under fast-flowing water to see how the water swirls the gravel around.

# Winding Rivers

Where the land is less steep, the river begins to flow more slowly, cutting sideways into the land rather than downward. The river now contains more water because other rivers and streams — called tributaries — have joined it, and it carries a greater load. The slower-moving water does not have enough power to carry all its load away, so some of the material drops to the river bed and settles there.

This meandering river looks brown and muddy because of all the sand and soil that it is carrying. A river drops more and more of its load as it slows down.

When a river flows slowly, the water travels around small humps or hillocks rather than rushing over them. This makes the river swing or meander from side to side.

levee

meander

# Do it yourself

**Work out the speed of a river's current and watch how water flows faster on the outside of a curve.**

Push two marker sticks into the river bank, about 300 feet (100 m) apart. Drop a twig into the water by one marker and time how long it takes to reach the other marker.

Watch how your twigs flow around curves. Where do they flow the fastest?

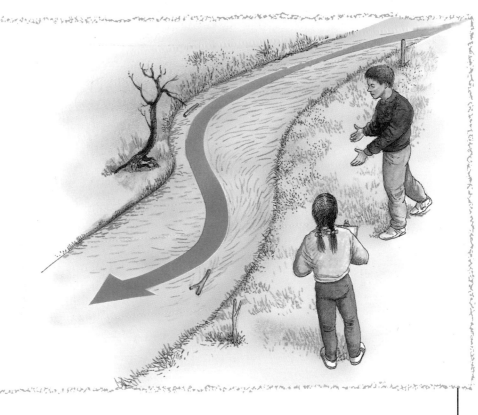

The wide, flat valley floor is called a floodplain. During a flood, the river may break through its banks, leaving behind gravel, sand, and mud, which build up in high banks called levees.

After a lot of rain, when there is more water in a river, the river may cut through the "neck" of a meander. This leaves behind a banana-shaped lake called an oxbow lake.

oxbow lake          floodplain

## Floods in China

The Huang He in China has flooded over 1,500 times since people began living there. In 1887, the flood was so bad that over one million people died.

## Winding Rivers

The point where a river meets the sea is called the river's mouth. Here, the river slows down even further, dropping more and more of its load. Deltas often form at river mouths when the material dropped by the river builds up into fan-shaped banks of new, flat land. The river splits into smaller channels, flowing around the new land to the sea.

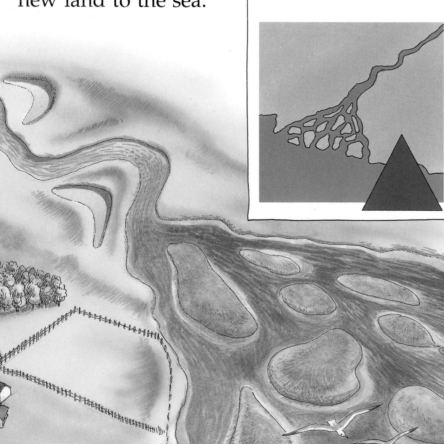

The new land made around a delta is almost flat. So when there is a lot of rain, rivers on deltas often break out of their channels and flood the land. Every year, many people living on the Ganges-Brahmaputra delta in Bangladesh are injured or even killed by heavy floods.

# The Nile

The world's longest river, the Nile, is actually made up of two rivers — the White Nile and the Blue Nile. Near the source of the river, at Lake Victoria, there are many rapids and waterfalls. Where the river joins the sea, 4,160 miles (6,695 km) away, there is a vast delta. In August and September, the Nile floods because of heavy rains near its source. The floodwaters used to spread rich soil over the farmers' fields in Egypt, but they are now held back behind the Aswan High Dam.

Farmers rely on the waters of the Nile to keep their crops alive. They use machines like this Archimedes screw to raise water from the river up to their fields.

Along the banks of the Nile in Egypt are two narrow green strips of land where crops are grown. Beyond is a dry and rocky desert.

## Aswan High Dam

The Aswan High Dam was built to control floods, provide a regular water supply, and help to make electricity.

# Lakes

Lakes are large hollows filled with rainwater, or the water from rivers or streams. They may be formed when glaciers, rivers, the wind, or movements deep inside the Earth create dips or channels in the land. Some lakes are made when water is held back by a barrier, such as the rocks left by glaciers or the hardened rock that once gushed out of volcanoes as liquid lava.

Although some of the world's lakes are huge, no lake lasts forever. They all eventually evaporate, fill with soil and plants or are drained by rivers.

Beavers may create a lake by building a dam of sticks and mud across a river. They then build their home, called a lodge, in the middle of the new lake, where it is safe.

Left: Rivers flowing into the Dead Sea, in the Middle East, carry so much salt from rocks high in the mountains that the lake's water is eight times saltier than sea water. People are able to float easily in such salty water.

Below: On the floor of the Great Rift Valley in East Africa is a chain of long, narrow, and deep lakes, including Lake Victoria, Lake Malawi, Lake Tanganyika, and Lake Nakuru. Lake Nakuru is famous for its thousands of beautiful pink flamingos.

## Loch Ness Monster?

Some people believe that the relatives of a huge pre-historic monster live in the deep waters of the Scottish lake, Loch Ness. But no one has been able to prove this by taking a clear photograph.

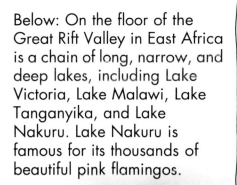

## Six Deepest Lakes

Lake Baikal in northern Asia is the world's deepest and oldest lake. It also contains the most water.

Baikal (5,315 ft.)

Tanganyika (4,710 ft.)

Caspian Sea (3,264 ft.)

Malawi/Nyasa (2,300 ft.)

Great Bear lake (1,348 ft.)

Superior (1,332 ft.)

# Oceans and Seas

Most of the world's water is contained in its five oceans – the Arctic, Atlantic, Indian, Pacific, and Southern (or Antarctic). Most of the Arctic Ocean is frozen and covered with ice. During the summer some of the ice melts, releasing huge blocks of drifting ice called pack ice, or smaller chunks called icebergs.

The world's seas are much smaller than the oceans. The seas are usually close to, or surrounded by, the Earth's land.

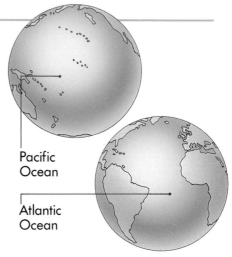

Pacific Ocean

Atlantic Ocean

The Pacific is the world's largest ocean — it is bigger than all the Earth's land put together.

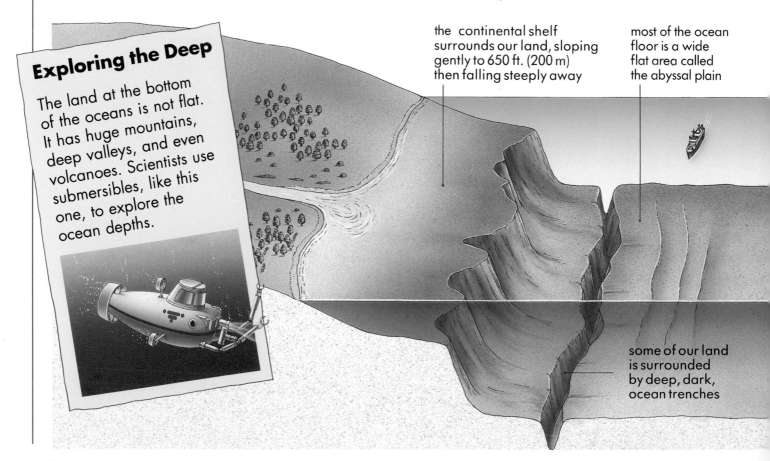

## Exploring the Deep

The land at the bottom of the oceans is not flat. It has huge mountains, deep valleys, and even volcanoes. Scientists use submersibles, like this one, to explore the ocean depths.

the continental shelf surrounds our land, sloping gently to 650 ft. (200 m) then falling steeply away

most of the ocean floor is a wide flat area called the abyssal plain

some of our land is surrounded by deep, dark, ocean trenches

# Do it yourself

**Make your own floating iceberg. All you need is a balloon, a bucket or a bowl — and some water!**

Follow the stages shown in the drawings. (Ask an adult to help you stretch the neck of the balloon over a cold faucet and knot the end when it is full of water.) See how much of your iceberg floats below the water's surface.

fill the balloon with water

cut the balloon away with scissors after the water has been frozen

the hidden part of an iceberg can be dangerous to ships

mountain ranges called mid-oceanic ridges run along parts of the ocean floor

some mountains break the ocean's surface to form island chains

# Deep Sea Fishes

The Sun's light and heat cannot reach deep down in the oceans, so it is dark and cold there. Many deep sea fishes, like this angler fish, produce their own light to help them find food.

# Waves, Currents, and Tides

The water in our seas and oceans is always moving, even when it looks calm and still. Winds blowing across the water make ripples, or waves, on the sea's surface, and create sweeping ocean currents. The level of the sea also rises and falls every day in a regular pattern of high and low tides. Tides are caused mainly by the pull of the Moon as it circles the Earth. Sometimes, huge waves called tsunamis are set off by underwater earthquakes and volcanoes.

A wave's size depends on the speed of the wind, and how long and how far the wind has been blowing.

## Eye-Spy

To see how waves work, try making some small waves in a bathtub and watch a bath toy, like a duck, bob up and down on a wave rather than moving forward.

## How Waves Work

In the open sea, waves look like they are traveling forward, but the water in each wave stays in almost the same place, moving around in circles. Near the shore, some of the water catches on the seabed. This slows the wave down and the top of the wave curves over and breaks.

crest      trough           breaking wave

## Ocean Currents

Ocean currents are like giant rivers, flowing slowly across the oceans and seas. There are nearly 40 main currents in the world's oceans. Warm currents, shown on this map in red, flow near the water's surface. They are created by winds. Cold currents, shown in green, are created when cold water sinks and spreads. They move deep down in the ocean depths.

At high tide, the sea rises up the shore, dumping seaweed, shells, feathers, wood, and other objects in a ragged line called the strandline.

Most coasts have two high tides and two low tides every 24 hours.

25

# Waves at Work

Waves carry with them the energy and power of the wind. Strong waves hurl rocks and pebbles against the coasts, wearing away cliffs. Breaking waves pound against rocks, squashing air into rock cracks. Then, when the waves pull back, the squashed air explodes out, weakening the rock and eventually breaking it apart. Cliff bases become worn away by the pounding waves until the upper parts overhang. This weakens the cliffs until large sections of rock may crumble into the sea.

Soft rocks, like chalk or limestone, wear away quickly. Houses built on soft cliffs may fall into the sea as the rocks beneath are cut away.

## Shaping the Coast

Soft rock is worn away to make bays, while hard rock juts out as headlands. Waves may punch a hole called a blowhole through the roof of a cave. Or caves on opposite sides of a headland may meet to form an arch. If the roof of an arch falls in, it leaves a column of rock called a stack.

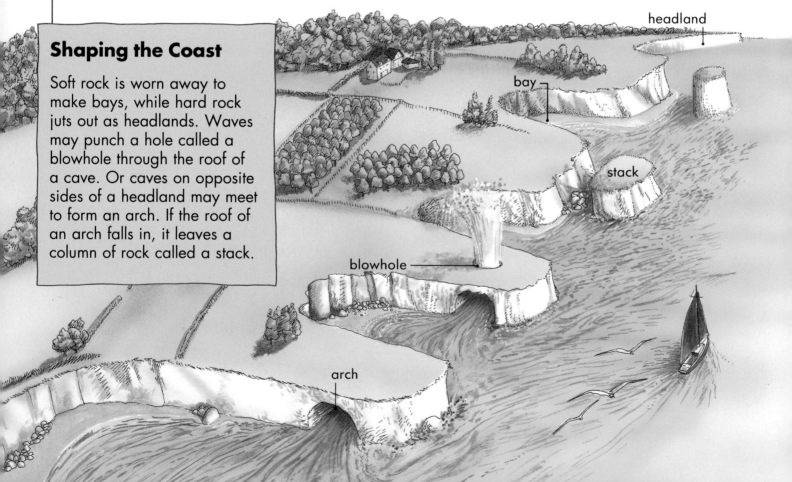

headland

bay

stack

blowhole

arch

# Do it yourself

**See how many different pebbles you can find if you visit the seashore. You may even spot pieces of semiprecious stones, such as jet, agate, and jasper.**

Look for pebbles that are different colors, shapes, and sizes. See if you can find any with holes right through. Some pebbles have colored bands of different rocks running through them. Others sparkle in the light.

There are many ways of sorting out your pebble collection. If you keep them in a clear container filled with water, the colors will show up well.

## Eye-Spy

As you suck a candy, it becomes smoother and rounder. In the same way, the rough edges of rocks become smooth as they roll around in the sea.

## More Things to Try

To make a pebble picture, draw a simple shape on a piece of thick cardboard. Sort out groups of small pebbles of the same size and color, glue them down and varnish them.

27

## Waves at Work

Sand, pebbles, and grains of rock and soil are washed onto our coasts by waves or dropped into the sea at river mouths. In sheltered areas, this material builds up to form beaches. On some beaches, the wind blows sand into small hills, or dunes. On headlands, sand may build up into a narrow ridge called a spit. The wind and waves can easily blow or wash away fine sand. To stop our coasts wearing away, people plant grasses, like marram grasses, or build fences, called groins.

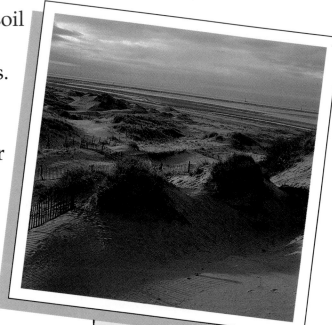

Marram grass grows quickly on sand dunes. Its roots bind the sand together and stop it from drifting away.

### Building a Spit

Where a coasts curves, waves may carry sand and pebbles on in a straight line, building a long ridge, or a spit.

spit

groin

### Longshore Drift

If waves hit a beach at an angle, they move the sand along in a zigzag path called longshore drift.

# Water Pollution

The Earth's water is much more polluted, or dirtier, than it used to be. Sewage, chemicals used on crops, and waste from factories are washed into rivers, lakes, and the oceans. And leaks and spills from oil tankers add to this pollution. Fishes and other creatures find it difficult to survive in polluted waters and this upsets the balance of life on Earth.

Pollution of the air, or atmosphere, may be heating the whole world. This could make the ice sheets at the poles melt, causing sea levels to rise and seawater to flood the land.

## Oil Damage

Oil sticks birds' feathers together so they cannot fly or swim — the birds will die unless their feathers can be cleaned.

This drawing shows some of the main causes of water pollution. We must stop polluting our rivers and oceans to avoid damaging people and wildlife all over the world.

garbage site

power station

farming

sewage plant

factory

mining

oil spillage from ships

# Do it yourself

## Make a water filter to clean up some dirty water.

**1.** Make some muddy water by mixing soil, sand, leaves, and twigs in an old container and pouring the mixture through a sieve.

**2.** Cut the bottom off a large plastic bottle and wedge some cotton batting in its neck.

**3.** Turn the bottle upside down and support it in a jar. Add a layer of gravel and sand over the cotton, then a sheet of blotting paper. These layers trap the dirt.

**4.** Pour the muddy water through the filter — but do not drink it. The filtered water is still very dirty!

soil, sand, leaves, and twigs

## 👁 Eye-Spy

Make a record of any water pollution near your home. Look out for garbage by river banks or shores and for oil or factory wastes floating on the water.

scum on side of bottle

blotting paper

glass to collect water

muddy water

sand

gravel

cotton batting

filtered water

# Amazing Rivers and Oceans

Although we know much more about the power of our rivers and oceans than people living long ago, the world under the sea is still a mysterious and dangerous place.

## Do it yourself

**Why not start a fact file about rivers and oceans?**

Divide your file into sections and use a ring binder so that you can add new pages to each section as you discover and learn more.

Collect postcards, stamps, and photographs and cut out pictures from magazines.

Scientists are still making exciting discoveries about the world under the sea, so look out for newspaper articles about new developments or undersea expeditions.

## Record Breakers

- Largest ocean — Pacific (64,100,000 sq. miles)
- Smallest ocean — Arctic (4,700,000 sq. miles)
- Deepest point on Earth — Mariana Trench, Pacific Ocean (36,198 ft. deep)
- Highest waterfall — Angel Falls, South America (3,212 ft.)
- Longest river — Nile (4,160 miles)
- Largest saltwater lake — Caspian Sea (143,244 sq. miles)
- Largest freshwater lake — Lake Superior, North America (31,700 sq. miles)
- Deepest lake — Lake Baikal, northern Asia (5,315 ft.)
- Highest sea wave ever recorded (111 ft. high)
- Longest glacier — Lambert-Fisher Ice Passage, Antarctica (250 miles long)
- Largest delta — Ganges-Brahmaputra (29,000 sq. miles)

# Index

abyssal plain 22
Antarctic Ocean 22
aquifer 8, 9
arch 26
Arctic Ocean 22, 31
Atlantic Ocean 22

Baikal, Lake 20, 31
beach 28

Caspian Sea 31
caves, on coasts 26
    underground 8
cliffs 26
coasts 25, 26, 28
condensation 6, 7
continental shelf 22
currents, ocean 24, 25

Dead Sea 20
delta 5, 18, 19, 31

evaporation 6

floodplain 17

glacier 4, 5, 10-11, 12, 20
groin 28

headland 26, 28

iceberg 4, 22, 23
impermeable rock 8, 9, 12
Indian Ocean 22
island 23

lake 5, 12, 20-21
levee 16
load 14, 16, 18
longshore drift 28

Mariana Trench 31
meander 4, 16, 17

Nile River 12, 19, 31

oasis 9
oceanic ridge
oxbow lake 17

Pacific Ocean 5, 22, 31

rainwater 6, 7, 12
rapids 14
river mouth 18, 28

seas 4, 5, 22
Southern Ocean 22
spit 28
spring 12
stack 26
stream 4, 10, 12, 13, 16

tide 24, 25
tributary 16
tsunami 24

valley 4, 10, 11, 14
Victoria, Lake 12, 19
volcano, undersea 22, 23

water table 8
water vapor 6
waterfall 14
waves 24, 26, 28